PINHOE
of Yester

Chips Barber

Sally Barber

OBELISK PUBLICATIONS

ALSO BY THE AUTHOR
The Lost City of Exeter / Great Little Exeter Book
Ghosts of Exeter / Beautiful Exeter
Topsham Past and Present
Around & About the Haldon Hills
Diary of a Dartmoor Walker / Diary of a Devonshire Walker
Great Little Dartmoor Book / Great Little Totnes Book
Made in Devon / Burgh Island and Bigbury Bay
Dark & Dastardly Dartmoor / Weird and Wonderful Dartmoor
Tales of the Teign / The Great Little Chagford Book
Ten Family Walks on Dartmoor / Ten Family Walks in East Devon
Great Little Plymouth Book / Plymouth in Colour
Ghastly and Ghostly Devon / Dawlish and Dawlish Warren
The South Hams / Beautiful Dartmoor
Torquay / Paignton / Brixham
Around & About Salcombe / Around & About Seaton and Beer
Around & About Sidmouth / Around & About Teignmouth and Shaldon
From the Dart to the Start / Dartmouth and Kingswear
Cranmere Pool – the First Dartmoor Letterbox
Brixham of Yesteryear
Teign Valley of Yesteryear

*For further details of these or any of our titles, please send an SAE to Obelisk
Publications at the address below, or telephone (01392) 468556*

*This book is dedicated to Daisy Reynolds,
without whom we would never have 'found' Pinhoe*

Acknowledgments
Many thanks to everyone who has kindly let me see and use their pictures of Pinhoe,
including Joe Rogers, Joan Rogers, Cyril Vinnicombe, Mr Potter, Ron Brealy, Ann
Webber, Ken and Jean Maun, Avril Spiller, Mrs Evelyn Lamacraft, Pat Peek, Mr Sid
Stamp, D. Clarke, Mr and Mrs David Pickford, G. Knight, Arthur Hitchcock, Pat Salter,
Mike Bennett, M. Martin, Mavis Piller, Mr Harris. I would also like to thank everyone
else who provided invaluable information but who are not specifically mentioned here
by name. Some of the 1950s photos are reproduced by kind courtesy of Express and Echo
Publications.

*First published in 1995 by
Obelisk Publications, 2 Church Hill, Pinhoe, Exeter, Devon
Designed by Chips and Sally Barber
Typeset by Sally Barber
Printed in Great Britain by
The Devonshire Press Limited, Torquay, Devon*

© Chips Barber/Obelisk Publications 1995

PINHOE

of Yesteryear

As a life-long Exonian, and Pinhoe resident of many years, I have written and researched many books about places all over Devon, but only ever included a fleeting glimpse of Pinhoe in *The Lost City of Exeter*. So it is with great pleasure that I embarked upon this project to present a portfolio of pictures of Pinhoe's people and places. There is no place quite like home!

I would like to thank all the people who so kindly either called in or invited me into their homes. I hope that the publication of this book has made all those cupboard searches, and attic assaults, worthwhile. Whilst I thank all the villagers who have lent pictures, if they are not included in this book, don't worry, for there are plans afoot for part 2!

We start with the group of people walking in procession from the centre of the village towards the Heart of Oak. On the left is the blacksmith's shop, where Mr Richard Quenton Rogers, better known as 'Dick', was the blacksmith. He succeeded his father in this role and was much sought after being exceedingly clever at his trade – there was little that was brought into that old smithy that 'Dick' could not tackle. His father had been the parish clerk and sexton for many years, and 'Dick' used to sing in the church choir. He was a veritable link with the past and was much missed by the Pinhoe folk and those who had business dealings with him when he passed away in December 1930 at 74 years of age. His business had been burnt out a few years previously in the disastrous fire of 1925, reported on the next few pages.

Pinhoe has suffered several times from fire and flood but certain episodes have been more dramatic than others, the fire of 1925 and the flood of June 1933 being two such notable occurrences. These events shattered the quiet existence of those who lived in Pinhoe, at a time when it really was a genuine country village, in its own right, and not simply a suburb of Exeter.

The fire was well covered in the local press and the following report is worth including for it gives a 'glowing' insight into the state of things in 1920s' Pinhoe.

Disastrous Fire at Pinhoe.
Six Cottages Burned And Twenty-Five People Homeless.

Damage to the extent of about £1,500 was caused yesterday at Pinhoe by a disastrous fire which gutted six cottages and rendered 25 people homeless. It is thought the thatch roof of the last of six cottages below the smithy, adjoining the main road on the Exeter side, became ignited by a spark from a passing engine. Within a short time of the discovery of the outbreak by a 'bus driver, the flames, fanned by a strong wind amounting to almost a gale, had involved six cottages, the smithy being also threatened. A great dash was made for furniture by two R.A.C. Scouts, P.C. Holman, and many villagers, but before the flames were extinguished several families had experienced great loss. They are being accommodated by friends in the village, and a subscription list—already well supported—has been opened on their behalf. Four families had their furniture insured, and the cottages, owned by Mr. Richard Quenton Rogers, were also insured with the Commercial Union.

It was a Devon General 'bus driver, named Luxton, who first discovered that the roof of the cottage occupied by Mr. Thomas Rogers, situated at the Exeter end of the row, was on fire. He informed Mrs. Rogers, while a passing motorist, who also noticed the fire, told P.C. Holman, the village constable, who was on duty at the five cross roads by Poltimore Arms. R.A.C. Supt. Paine and Patrol Cotton ran down with fire extinguishers, with which they are supplied for use in case of motor fires, while P.C. Holman also proceeded to the scene of the outbreak. Luxton procured his fire extinguisher, and it seemed as if the fire, which was only confined to a tiny patch at that time, would be easily extinguished. A sudden gust of wind from the south-west, however, fanned the flames along the thatch of the bottom three cottages, and the roofs were almost immediately a blazing inferno. Above the three thatched cottages were two slated ones, but the fire bridged this obstacle and caught the thatch of a cottage higher up. Here, however, a gap was presented by the low smithy, and the new brick houses above were in almost perfect immunity.

Seeing the houses were doomed, P.C. Holman gave orders for the removal of the furniture. In this operation assistance was rendered by the villagers, including many women, prominent helpers being Messrs. Tapley, Tracey, Rudd, Stiles, Burns, sen. and jun., Westcott, White, Burgess, and Good. The police present were P.C.'s Holman, White, Brewer and Carter, while Sergt. Ridd, of Alphington, also came on the scene. Great praise has been bestowed on P.C. Holman and the two R.A.C. men, who worked like trojans to save the goods and chattels of the unfortunate people involved. Their task was by no

means easy. Owing to the smallness of the rooms haste was impossible, but many articles were nevertheless, salved and placed either in the roadway or in Mr. T. Rogers's yard opposite. The main road resembled a fair; pillows and bedding were thrown from the windows, but with articles the rescuers were not so lucky. For example, a birch wardrobe stuck when it was being forced through the window, and there it had to be left and was burned.

Almost as soon as the outbreak was discovered P.C. Holman had requested R.A.C. Patrol Cotton to telephone for the Exeter Fire Brigade, but before its arrival the roofs of five cottages had fallen in, sending up volumes of smoke and flames, while the sixth cottage was well alight. Even then great progress in fighting the fire was rendered impossible by an inadequacy of water, which was the subject of biting comment. Only two hydrants could be used, and there was no pressure behind the water, which comes from Exeter, although the Poltimore supply had been cut off. The motor fire engine was stationed outside the Poltimore Arms, and three lengths of hose were employed, but the force and quantity of water was pitifully inadequate. The sixth cottage became well alight, and burned furiously, the portion of the row resisting the fire most being two brick and slated cottages in the centre.

The end cottage, which caught first, was razed almost to the ground. Of the next two, portions of cob walls alone remained, with blackened floor joists supporting the twisted remains of bedsteads hanging precariously between them. These three cottages were all of cob and thatch, the latter material causing great anxiety to the firemen, who laboured hard to dig it away. Jets of water were occasionally directed on the end of a row of four thatched cottages to the west of the burning buildings, which frequently became hot to the point of ignition. The wind, however, kept the flames away from these cottages to a great extent. They are occupied by Messrs. Stamp and Woodley (2), and Mrs. Mears, and fortunately escaped with no injury. Had the fire developed towards the north, practically the whole village would have been doomed, for with the limited amount of water, supplied by a three inch main only, it would have been impossible to check the flames.

The families rendered homeless are: No. 1, Thomas Rogers, his wife, and seven children; No. 2, Ernest May, wife, and two children; No. 3, William Henry Spry and wife; No. 4, Mrs. Mary Greenslade (widow) and her niece (Miss Rowe); No. 5, Mrs. Elizabeth Ruth Gay, an invalid widow; No. 6, Richard Q. Rogers, owner of the cottages, Mr. and Mrs. Hooper, and four nieces. Mr. T. Rogers was only partly insured, and Mr. Spry and Mrs. Gay were not insured. The heaviest sufferer was, probably, Mr. Rogers, who was away at Cullompton when the outbreak occurred. Most of his furniture was destroyed, and he has the largest family. His articles which were saved-mostly kitchen goods-were removed to his premises across the road. Hardly any bedroom furniture was rescued, and Mr. Rogers lost even his overcoat. Mrs. Rogers said she was indoors, sitting down, when the 'bus driver told her the house was on fire. She went out, but it was only a small patch-no bigger than a man's hand. She had a baby in her arms at the time. Mr. Rogers, who has lived in the cottage all his life, was very philosophical about his loss. The house was old, he said, and out of evil came good.

Mrs. Gay said she was in her back garden at the time of the outbreak, and saw fire at the base of Mr. Rogers's chimney. She started removing furniture upstairs, but lost a lot, including a new wardrobe and two dressers.

Mrs. Greenslade was out at the time of the outbreak, and her front door was forced by the helpers in order to remove her furniture.

R.A.C. Patrol Cotton, after working to get out furniture, went on duty at the cross-roads and diverted the heavy stream of traffic to Exeter by another route, the hose, fire engine, and furniture combining to make the main Exeter-road at Pinhoe almost impassable.

Mr A.T. Dew of Monkerton Manor, offered sleeping accommodation as well as Mr. L.R. Collins, of Landour House, who also provided food. Furniture was stored in Mr. England's garage and at Monkerton Farm, through the kindness of Mr. G. Howe. Mr. Richard Rogers and his family slept at Mr. Yelland's house. The subscription list is in the hands of the Vicar and Mr. F. Jones.

The flood, one of many to inundate Pinhoe, occurred some eight years afterwards and was a spectacle for those who didn't suffer hardship from it. A thunderstorm broke over the high ground that lies between Pinhoe and Stoke Canon, between 3.30 p.m. and 6.30 p.m. on a hot and humid late June afternoon. The skies lit up with terrific streaks of lightning and great claps of thunder sent young ones, and those of a nervous disposition, scurrying beneath tables and other objects to escape the awesome conditions that prevailed at the storm's height. With it were two rainstorms, the like of which had rarely been experienced in the district and millions of gallons of precipitation came cascading down on a Pinhoe populace that could do little but sit and watch in awe at the ferocity of it all. To add to all this a storm of giant hail stones forced people off the streets for several minutes as their impact pinged peoples' ears inflicting great pain.

The headlines in the next day's papers said: "Three families homeless—Trains held up as sleepers washed away—Residents seek refuge in upper rooms." Newspaper reports told of how a flood of water descended Church Hill, making it look more like a river than a road. As waves of water descended this steep hill, large accumulations of stones and pebbles were swept along with it. The cottages at the bottom temporarily impeded the flow, the waters rising to the fifth step in some properties. The pressure of the flood waters was so great that heavy manhole covers were thrust several feet into the air.

The waters raged on down Station Road. A similar thing happened on Gipsy Hill, those living down near the Pin Brook being inundated from all directions. In the same cloudburst there were problems right the way from Stoke Canon, through Huxham, Poltimore and on down to Clyst St Mary. The Headmistress of the long defunct Poltimore Girls' College, told newspaper reporters that, "I have never seen rain like it before. Poltimore Park looks like a lake with water two feet deep right across it."

The Heart of Oak, featured at different times in these four views, is one of a few thatched pubs in the Exeter area, other notable ones being found in Heavitree and Exwick. For a day or two, in early September 1986, it temporarily changed its name to "A Place in the Sun" when it became a prize in a national newspaper. "Locals" were shipped in, looking more trendy than some of the usual regulars. A television commercial was made, the pub being spruced up to look like the 'idyllic, beautiful, country pub' that the promoting newspaper claimed to be offering as a prize in a phone-in competition where you had to hear a question, each day, for five consecutive days before ringing in with the answers – a nice little earner! The words used to portray the inn stated that, "It has a thatched roof and roses round the door." However a rival newspaper described the Heart of Oak as "a paint-peeling local, hard by a busy road with a mouldy thatched roof and tightfisted locals.' The literary and verbal banter got a bit out of hand and, as it eventually transpired, the winner

chose not to take up the option of the pub's lease, combined with several other goodies, instead taking the alternative cash prize. The promotion brought some famous faces to Pinhoe. Present were the legendary snooker player, Alex 'Hurricane' Higgins, darts champion, Eric Bristow and 'Page 3' girls Davina Laurie, Angie Layne and Linda Lusardi. One of the more unusual attractions of the TV-portrayed Pinhoe pub was the beer garden on the main road! It's amazing what a few clever camera angles can achieve!

Above is the building now known as The White House, just a stone's throw along the road from the Heart of Oak towards Venny Bridge. This was the police house, the sign above the door can be used in evidence! Outside is stood Julia Potter with her younger sister, Joyce. Below, the picture of the Jubilee Club's outing is taken on the slope near the present library. Looking towards Pinhoe, the only building is in the distance. This was Pinhoe's school, which was set back a short distance from Main Road where BT now have premises. The view is totally unimpaired by any buildings at Oak Close or beyond. The thin line that runs below the distant school is the bottom end of Church Hill today.

Above is a view of what is now Venny Bridge, the road that runs in a curve parallel to Pinhoe Road. This was taken when there were only a small number of cottages close to the junction of Chancel Lane. These were demolished some years ago and now houses occupy both sides of the road.

Below is an aerial photo that shows Pinhoe Road quite clearly. There have been many changes – some additions, like Great Mills, and some notable losses, like the Pinhoe grain silo demolished in November 1989. There were times, in its heyday, when lorries tailed back a long way to off-load their grain here.

This is the centre of Pinhoe, a place that now has two mini-roundabouts and sees a continuous flow of traffic all day long. Not much of the scene above remains. Freddie Patch's garage, on the corner of Church Hill and the main road, moved a little way down the road towards the Heart of Oak. The RAC box has long gone as has its keeper, Charlie Cotton, who directed traffic across the junction. The building on the left corner, opposite the garage, was once a shop that sold porcelain and gift items run by Twiggs. In a different time it was also Mrs Shute's tea room, a reminder that nothing is permanent! There are some newspaper hoardings outside the shop in the left foreground. This newsagent was run by Tabitha Patch, Freddie Patch's wife and in later years it became Lockhart's. The picture below is almost the reverse view looking from outside the Hall Church towards the centre of the village. The Poltimore Arms can be seen on the right.

The pub is also prominent in these two pictures. There was far less traffic in the days when these were taken, there also being no need to protect pedestrians with railings then. Creedy Valley Cider is clearly advertised, and there is even an extra exit to stagger out of on the Langaton Lane side of the pub! The board, close to the corner, is the bus timetable.

The buildings on the right of the bottom picture have long since gone, to be replaced by one of Pinhoe's two friendly supermarkets. It's rumoured that a former Lord Poltimore disapproved of the licensed premises at Poltimore village because he didn't like his men going to church in a drunken state. Therefore the pub's status was removed to Pinhoe along with the name. Originally it was called the Bampfylde Arms, the family name of Lord Poltimore, who had lands and property in a lot of places in the region.

The picture above shows Church Hill, in a time when it was a much narrower and quieter thoroughfare than it is now. Close observation of the picture shows that Joe Rogers' hardware shop doesn't exist yet, it being just a space. There are no pavements up Church Hill, but there probably didn't need to be any then. All the houses had longer front gardens, but these were foreshortened when the road was widened.

If you look, very closely, at the runners taking the bend in the picture below, you might spot Jimmy Savile! At the time his brother was stationed at the Royal Marine Camp at Lympstone. A keen marathon runner, Sir Jimmy was welcomed by the organisers of Exeter's event, a famous name always helping to raise the profile of a charity event.

Now take a close look at the top picture opposite. This compact, detached building 'grew up' to become the premises of the Spar Shop in Pinhoe, but when this picture was taken, in about 1930, it was Freddie Pyle's 'Model Dairy'. You will see that the building is only a fraction of its present size, a window count of the upper storey showing just how much smaller. Either side there is open space – very different from today's much enlarged shop.

In the lower, but much later, picture there appears to be a paved approach to the original shop entrance. The street furniture is very different today, the old-fashioned

direction post, where the railings are now, has given way to modern signing. However, it's amazing how many people still stop to ask for directions! The signpost would have labelled the main road as the A38 but the road has since been reclassified as the B3181. At one time it was the busiest road in the country!

Overleaf, the centre pages show a revealing aerial view of Pinhoe, and it really is up to you to spot the changes. It's taken before the Causey Gardens/Playmoor Drive houses were built as the glasshouses of Playmoor Nursery occupy the centre foreground. There are cottages between the Pinhoe Garage and the bank. The old Pinhoe School can be seen on the right and the new one can be seen on the left! Several cottages have now gone and new roads, like Bickleigh Close amongst others, have yet to be built.

Pinhoe

Pinhoe

Here is the junction of Danesway and Church Hill. Although the left side of the picture is very dark and shadowy, it's still possible to see how narrow it was, indeed in keeping with the rest of the width up the hill towards Stoke Canon and with that of Harrington Lane. Many of the buildings in this vicinity, including most of the houses in Church Hill up to the junction with Harrington Lane, Danesway and buildings along the road towards Broadclyst, were the work of a building firm called Loman's. They had started in Exeter by building houses in Buddle Lane and Hamlin Lane. Following their success they moved to Pinhoe where they were kept busy for several years right through the 1930s.

The middle picture shows Church Hill looking up the hill from just above the shops.

Harrington Lane will never look like this again! It shows the lane between the junction of Bradfield Road and Chancel Lane. Imagine the traffic snarl-ups today if the lane had kept its original width! In the past even the limited amount of traffic that used this lane could not go all the way to the bottom of Stoke Hill as Prince Charles Road is a relatively modern thoroughfare, dating back to just after the Second World War. Travellers would have to descend to Polsloe Bridge to get past the railway line, as there was no other direct access to the city.

Perhaps these instantly recognisable Station Road scenes haven't changed too much but a pavement, advertising signs and other, more subtle changes have occurred. The vehicle in the picture gives some idea that this picture was taken many decades ago.

The post office is shown where the Cottrells have been associated with Pinhoe for a great number of years.

There also used to be a bakery nearby and there are still some of the older Pinhoe residents who have fond memories of shopping there, who recall the wonderful smell of fresh, newly-baked bread.

On the opposite side of the road is a launderette that was once a dairy run by Tommy Rudd.

Here we have two pictures looking the other way up Station Road.

For many years there were houses only on one side of this section of Station Road. Opposite the houses was an open space, called Station Meadow, where the landowner, Mr Burrows, allowed children to play their games in safety. This space was at the back of the Heart of Oak, where much of Oakley Close is today. Mr Burrows had a garage in Exmouth. The pictures show part of the evolution of this thoroughfare as a residential one for the older top picture has no pavements and not much of a road surface whereas the lower one does. Neither has much in the way of parked cars — the chances of taking such a vehicle-free picture like this again are probably less than winning first prize in the National Lottery!

Pinhoe's railway station has had its moments and has experienced a chequered history. At one time it had much more importance than today, with several members of staff employed. There were more buildings, including a booking office on the up line side and, not only a general waiting room, complete with glowing embers in winter time, but also another just for the ladies.

Originally there was an attractive timber bridge, almost opposite the present day Pinhoe Surgery, linking the two platforms. In the late 1920s this was removed to be replaced by one made of concrete. Some say that this was the first of its kind used by any railway in this country.

One of the former signalmen at Pinhoe Station was Mr Parker. If he was on duty all night he would fill the wee small hours by knitting pairs of woollen socks!

Below is a more modern picture taken on 16 May 1983, the day that Pinhoe's station was reopened after years of simply watching the trains whistle through. It was taken from the top of the slide in the children's play area in the park. It was a wet Monday, but this didn't dampen the enthusiasm of the children who were invited to ride the train to St David's station, before being 'bussed' back to Pinhoe school.

The Gipsy Hill Hotel sits on top of a ridge that looks northwards towards the village, shown here several decades ago when it was a much smaller hotel.

Below is a picture of the male members of the Pinhoe Branch of the British Legion. From left to right, back row: E. Woodley, W.B. Smith, L.B. Butt, W.G. Joslin, R. Sleet, J. Peters, C. Holden, W. Turner, H. Hill, C. Burns. 3rd row: G. Hallett, C. Burgess, H. Chave, W.J. Nute, J. Way, E. May, A.E. Snow, W. Ford, F. Johns, W.J. Sandford, A. Smith. 2nd row: A. Reeves, G. Coldridge, W.G. May, H. Perry, W.C. Harris, B. Maunder, H.W. Snell, H.A. Roberts, A. Ireland, F.D. Ford, W. Spry, A. Fone, P. Tracy. Front row: W.H. Allway, B. Griffen DCM, A. Dommett, Major S.E. Odgers MC (Hon. Sec. and Treasurer), R.S. Lang (Vice President), Major W.S. Nicholson RA (Vice President), Col. O.M. Harris DSO RA, Lt. A.T. Dew RN (President), W.G. Willis-Watson (Vice Chairman), Col. R.W.H. Middlemass (Vice President), Rev. O. Puckridge, T.L. Reynolds, W.J. Way, W.C. Fone. They are pictured here at Monkerton Manor, on 8 April 1933.

They don't make hayricks like this any more! This photo features Ernest May working at the Odgers' farm. The field where this photo was taken is now covered by the large housing development at Monkerton. Mr May's first job, on leaving school, at a tender age, was scaring crows with a rattle.

Below is an assembly that includes many Pinhoe personnel.

Here we have a few pictures taken in the Temporary Hall, so called because it was built in 1948 to be used for a period of five years – but survived to serve the community for a bit longer than that. It was located near the stream at Monkerton and provided a venue for a number of activities. In this picture a meal is being enjoyed by a large number of local people who have, mostly, turned to pose for the photographer. Although we can't name everyone who is present we know that Major Hext is there along with his wife. Amongst others who have been identified are Mr Loman, Mr Potter, Mr and Mrs Woodley and Mr Scoble.

The Temporary Hall was used for a range of activities as these pictures demonstrate so well. Christmas and party balloons are the order of the day for the top picture whilst a fancy dress party has stretched the resources of many Pinhoe parents to turn their children into a variety of colourful characters. In the lower picture most of the children have answered the call of the photographer but alas the good fairy has turned away at the crucial moment.

Brookfield, a large house a few yards to the south of Pinhoe's railway station, was the venue for an urgent meeting for members of the Pinhoe Village Drama Club on 6 May

1951. Certain members of the cast were told to 'get their act together' as some of them still hadn't learnt their lines for the production of *Prunella*. However, the show was eventually staged, a month later, in The Temporary Hall and, as can be seen, the set made good use of extremely limited facilities. The producer was the celebrated Ian Kelway. The press regarded his production of this play, shown on the top of page 25, as a brave venture, audiences of a hundred being treated to the very first production of the group. Cramped into the smallest of venues, a cast of 23, backed up by 12 production assistants, interpreted this fantasy play, written by Laurence Housman and Harley Granville Barker, in a 'delightful' way. The stage was so small that as soon as anyone stepped off the stage they were immediately on the grass outside the hall! People involved in this production included Jean Flood, Agnes Sleet, Pamela Bindon, Margaret Bindon, Flora Orton, Marion Orton, Cedric Marshall, Evelyn D. Rogers, Yvonne Rogers, Barbara Harris, Susan Harris, Beryl Shepherd, I. Harris, John Harris, Ann Winsor, Pauline Lyons, Dorothy Smith, Sylvia Vincent, Michael Pope and Sydney Eddy.
The sequence of pictures on these pages features a range of performances.

The More the Merrier, a comedy by Ronald Millar, was staged at America Hall between 19-21 October 1972. Shown in the picture at the bottom of page 25 are the leading members of that production. Back row (L to R): Colin Davey, Jill Chettle, Jeffrey Pearson, Rhoda Gumm, Dorothy Smith. Front row: Marianne Roberts, Ann Webber, Arthur Harris and Malcolm Roberts.

A year later and the production this time was *The Camel's Back*, as shown by the picture below. From left to right: John Jenkin, Agnes Sleet, Gerry Norburn, Ann Webber, Jean Wilson, Dorothy Smith and Jillian Chettle.

The group managed to continue their productions through to celebrate their 40th Anniversary in April 1991 but there was never going to be a 50th! Sadly the last play to be staged was in November 1992 when the final curtain was brought down on a band of players who brought immense entertainment to the local populace.

The Rev. Puckridge, Vicar of Pinhoe for 41 years, was noted for his cycling daredevil exploits, in particular descending Church Hill at an alarming speed only to brake at the very last moment on reaching the bottom.

By all accounts he was an amazing man, noted for his musical ability, as an authority on Pinhoe's history, a talented, all round sportsman who grew increasingly eccentric as the years rolled by. His wife passed away at the end of 1943 and he died a few days later. Rev. Puckridge is attributed with naming the trees, shown here, the "twelve apostles".

The bells! The bells! These were reinstalled in the church in the early 1950s. Shown in the top picture are Rev. Matthews, Fred Pyle and Bill Stamp.

On this pair of pages we have four teams, two of choirboys and two soccer teams. The date given on the back of the top picture says 1909, so a good few hymns and psalms have been sung since then!

The top photo shows the Pinhoe team of 1910/11 but with no trophies to show off – unlike the team of a decade later. The bottom photograph shows the members of Pinhoe AFC's cup-winning team of the early 1920s. In the 1920/21 season they lifted the Football Express Cup and the following season they went on to win the East Devon Cup. The personnel of the 1921/22 team are named as follows: Back row (L to R): T. Rudd, W. Joslin, W.J. Lang (Hon Treas), W. Enticott, J. Bussell, F. Coles. Middle row: R. Simpson, J. Squires, A. Potter, J. Stoneman, D. Stoneman, H. Bindon, G. Bauer. Front row: Mr W.J. Heywood (Chairman), R. Powell, W. Potter, R. Bray (Captain), L. Bray, F. Bailey, W.J. Powell (Hon. Sec.).

We come to the end of our look back at Pinhoe of Yesteryear with two very different pictures. The top one shows the Rifle Club at an Annual Dinner at America Hall, whilst the bottom one shows an award-winning float from Pinhoe Carnival in the early years of the twentieth century.